Contents

INTRODUCTION

CHAPTER ONE: The Draw   1

CHAPTER TWO: The Damage   14

CHAPTER THREE: Other Risks   27

CHAPTER FOUR: Other Smokers   41

CHAPTER FIVE: Dealing with Temptation   57

CHAPTER SIX: So you want to Quit?   70

CHAPTER SEVEN: Stopping Strategies   88

CHAPTER EIGHT: Staying Smoke Free   102

USEFUL CONTACTS   117

INDEX   118

Other essential

BULLYING
Michele Elliott

DIVORCE AND SEPARATION
Matthew Whyman

DRUGS
Anita Naik

EATING
Anita Naik

PERIODS
Charlotte Owen

SELF-ESTEEM
Anita Naik

SEX
Anita Naik

SMOKING
Matthew Whyman

SPOTS
Anita Naik

YOUR RIGHTS
Anita Naik

See page 120 for more details.

Introduction

Cigarettes: some can't live with the habit, others think they can't live without it. I used to light up on a regular basis. Compared to my mates, however, I was a late starter. At 15, I was one of the few people who didn't vanish for a crafty smoke every break time. Then I fell for a girl who puffed away like a factory chimney, and I was tempted to take up the habit so I could join her in the smoking circle.

By the time I discovered that she wouldn't date me if I was the last guy on earth, it was way too late. I was hooked, and a whole decade passed before I finally succeeded in quitting.

I didn't worry about the health risks at the time. Who does? At that age, you think you'll live forever. Besides, I quite enjoyed filling my lungs with smoke ten times a day. What really worried me was that my mum would suss me. If she ever found out, I feared she'd kill me faster than any tobacco habit.

In a bid to steer clear of her, I mastered the art of secret smoking. This involved 'popping out to post a letter' half a dozen times a day, dragging down a fag as if I were dependent on the tube for oxygen, then coming home stinking of mints. At night, providing the breeze was favourable, you could find me leaning dangerously from my bedroom window, all for the sake of a ciggie. Either way, I was risking life and limb.

Sad, I know. At the time, however, as a fully paid-up member of the nicotine-dependency club, it seemed to me like perfectly reasonable behaviour. Smoking was a way of life. A trusty marker that defined each day. It only became a major problem when I first tried to go without.

Giving up is never easy. It took me the best part of forever. I tried everything. From plastering myself with nicotine patches to sprint-smoking until I was sick. Neither method worked for me. My addiction was too far gone.

Or so I thought.

In the end, I gave up feeling helpless and started getting angry. My life was ruled by the need to spark up. I had become a slave to cigarettes. I wished I had never started in the first place. Curiously, the bitterness I felt about letting myself get into this situation actually worked in my favour. It was enough to spark the willpower I so badly needed to bin my final pack of smokes.

Beating one of life's most addictive habits is a buzz. It boosts your confidence and self-esteem. Even so, I still have my wobbly moments. People who tell you giving up is a cinch are basically aliens. It takes bags of determination to stub out the habit and stay smoke-free. Anyone can do it, but you really have to want to quit.

Whatever your attitude towards smoking, here's a guide that sets the myths alight and leaves you with the burning facts. You won't find any guaranteed ways to give up or avoid giving in. Just the info and advice to help you make informed decisions about every aspect of the smoking issue – from the impact on your lungs to your lifestyle and your wallet.

Matteo

The Draw

"I always look forward to the first cigarette of the day, even though it makes me feel sick."

Greg, 15

"I never used to smoke during the week. I started by having one or two at a party, just to be sociable. Somehow, the habit just quickly caught up on me."

Sophie, 16

"The more people say you shouldn't smoke, the more tempting it is to go out and spark one up. It's all part of the attraction."

Isla, 14

WHY DO SOME PEOPLE SMOKE?

What is it about sucking on a smouldering tube of tobacco that gets over a quarter of the population lighting up on a regular basis by the time they're fifteen? The fact that it'll seriously screw up your health can't be much of an attraction. Nor the fact that it costs a small fortune, and makes your breath smell worse than a dog's bottom. There has to be *something*, however, so what's the draw?

The fact is every smoker will give you a different answer. Different people light up for different reasons. Here are some of the most influential factors:

Mood control

Smoking tobacco has a stimulating effect on the body. At the same time, it works on certain areas of the brain as a relaxant. This is why sometimes people reach for the cigarettes to stay alert, and at other times to keep calm, relieve stress or to help them unwind in social situations.

"During revision for my GCSE's, I smoked more cigarettes than ever before. I'd take a break every hour, step outside with a cup of tea and get through two smokes before going back to my books. I looked forward to lighting up, it got me through the work, but cutting down afterwards wasn't easy. It became a habit which I still haven't got under control."

Jo, 16

Recent research shows that men are more likely to smoke to control their emotions than women, especially if they feel angry or sad. Unlike girls, so the theory goes, boys aren't encouraged to talk about their feelings, and share them with others. Somehow, it's seen as being unmacho. As a result, they find physical ways to express themselves. Anything from starting a fight to striking up a smoke!

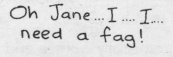

Oh Jane... I .... I.... need a fag!

"I definitely smoke more when I'm wound up.
The trouble is I don't live near any shops, so when I'm
uptight and out of cigarettes it just makes me feel
even more tense!"

Obi, 15

"If I'm feeling down or depressed, a cigarette takes
my mind off the problem. It makes me feel better."

Jack, 16

BURNING FACT:

*In a recent survey, 17% of smokers planned to drop
out before taking their GCSEs, compared to just 10%
of non-smokers. So smoking gives you confidence, eh?*

The weight myth

Many people, especially women and girls, buy into
the belief that smoking keeps their weight down, or
even helps them to slim. This is basically a myth, and
a dangerous one at that.

"My older sister's obsessed with looking good. Weight
is one of her major hang-ups, and she's really careful
about what she eats. The crazy thing is she won't give
up smoking because she's scared she'll balloon. It's
like her figure is more important to her than a long,
healthy life."

Helen, 14

Nicotine may well take the edge from your appetite, but people who pack in smoking don't automatically pack on the pounds. Any weight gain is down to the fact that they tend to eat more as a substitute for smoking. So when you're giving up, and looking for a way to avoid reaching for a cigarette, go for something other than the fridge! Ultimately, if you really have to snack to beat the craving, choose healthy, low-fat foods. That way, the only pounds you'll put on are those you stash in your pocket.

BURNING FACT:

Approximately one tree in every 25, cut down throughout the world, is burnt to cure tobacco and make it ready for smoking.

The smoking lifestyle

Some people get into the smoking habit because it's widely perceived to be an act of sophistication or rebellion. In fact recent surveys suggest that nearly 40% of young people believe smokers are less likely to conform than those who choose to stay smoke free. It's a tempting image. One which has long been manipulated by the media to reinforce certain ideas, attitudes and beliefs.

"It's always the bad guys who smoke in the movies."
Regis, 14

"The best adverts are always for cigarettes. Either they're really funny or dead clever."

Charli, 13

"When an actor, a model or a pop star is photographed with a cigarette, it's bound to have an impression on your average teenager."

James, 15

The influence of the media on your attitude to smoking is very hard to prove. There may not be a direct link, but regular exposure over a long period of time is difficult to ignore.

BURNING FACT:

Nearly 500 million people alive today will eventually die from smoking-related diseases.

Joining the pack

There's a big difference between being unique and feeling excluded. No matter how much pride you take in being an individual, it's easy to feel left out when everyone else is lighting up.

> "I used to go to my local skate club after school each day. There was a real vibe about the place, a kind of group bond among the skaters. So when the ciggies were passed around, I always took one because I didn't want to look like the odd one out. It used to make me cough and feel sick, but I couldn't say no after the first one. Not without looking like a total lightweight!"
>
> Rick, 15

Experts reckon your friends are the single most important factor that determines whether you'll ever spark up a ciggie. If a mate smokes, then chances are you'll be tempted to follow their lead. Peer pressure can be a powerful force in all areas of teenage life. No-one can tell you to ignore it. Resistance has to come from within. Ultimately, much depends on your self-esteem. If you feel confident in yourself, and the image you give out, then you're less likely to do things like try a cigarette simply because someone you admire says you should.

> "If I'm talking to a guy I fancy, then I always feel the need to light up. I just feel more comfortable with a cigarette in my hand, and I like to watch the smoke when I exhale."
>
> Carol, 16

"I'm not stupid. I know that I smoke at parties because it makes me feel less twitchy. I wish I could rise above it, but the temptation is so difficult to resist."

William, 15

BURNING FACT:

One puff on a ciggie delivers over 4,000 different chemicals into your body. Many are known to cause cancer.

Your background

Some people grow up in a home environment where the air is so thick with smoke it's virtually impossible to see the telly.

Living with a smoker is likely to influence your opinion on the habit, but there are no guarantees which way you'll swing. Some react against it, others fall into the same habits.

"Both my mum and dad are smokers. They were cross when my older brother took up the habit, but they hadn't exactly set the perfect example!"

Maria, 13

BURNING FACT:

Christopher Columbus first introduced the world to tobacco in 1492, having come across Native Americans rolling their own for ceremonies. When the habit took off, millions of Africans were shipped to America as slaves to help grow the crop for profit.

"My dad's been trying to give up smoking ever since I was born. Every New Year he gives it a go, but within a week he's puffing away again. It would be funny if I wasn't so worried that it's going to kill him in the end. Seeing how hard it is to stop has certainly persuaded me never to touch a cigarette. Most of my friends smoke, but they're going to be in for a shock when they realise how addictive it can be."

Sonya, 14

The addiction factor

Scientists are still at odds with the tobacco industry about whether nicotine should be classed as an addictive substance. Away from the debate, however, the majority of smokers will tell you how easy is to get hooked on the habit. Here's why:

- It's possible to become psychologically dependent on anything you do on a regular basis to change your mood. When it comes to cigarettes, this means you keep lighting up because you feel that you can't manage without a smoke.
- Nicotine is one of the only drugs you can consume at the same time as doing other activities. This makes it much easier to develop a smoking habit.
- Nicotine has a direct effect on the way your brain functions. It effectively reprogrammes your mind to make you believe that you need nicotine in order to function normally.
- Becoming dependent on cigarettes doesn't happen overnight. For the majority of people, the first few cigarettes are really unpleasant. This is because the

nicotine hasn't had a chance to fully rewire the mind. It only takes a few more fags for the task to be complete. Only then does the habit become a problem, because you realise you can't quit so easily.

"You don't have to halt what you're doing to smoke a fag. What's more, it doesn't change the way you think or act like alcohol. The nicotine effect is far more subtle, which is what makes it so horribly habit forming."

Jake, 15

"When you smoke your first cigarette, it's easy to think you'll never get hooked. It tastes so disgusting, you wonder what all the fuss is about."

Astrid, 14

BURNING FACT:

All around the world, 6,000,000,000,000 cigarettes are smoked each year.

REAL LIFE

Mark, 16, never considered himself to be a smoker, until his new girlfriend asked him to go without:

"I hated my first cigarette. It tasted disgusting, and I couldn't understand how someone would willingly want to smoke. A few days later I tried it again. I guess I was just curious, and all my mates seemed to enjoy it. I managed to finish it without coughing, even though I ended up feeling as ropy as I had the first time. After that I didn't smoke for a week, but then I went to a party and the ciggies came out. This time I sparked one up no problem. I felt like I knew what I was doing, plus it stopped me feeling like a spare part when everyone else was smoking around me. I ended up cadging so many from my friends, however, that I realised I was going to have to buy my own."

GROUNDED

"That night, just after I got home, I was sick twice. My clothes stunk like an ashtray, and my dad grounded me for a week. He was onto me straight away, but I found it hard to take any grief from him because he used to be a smoker himself. Meanwhile, my mum reacted as if I'd signed my own death warrant. She went well overboard, and it just made me more determined to smoke again. Looking back, I can see they were just concerned. Even so, it felt as if they were trying to tell me how to live my life."

THE BUZZ

"I bought my first packet of cigarettes that week, and smoked the odd one whenever my folks went out. When I ran out, I bought some more straight away. It didn't feel like an expensive habit, but at that point the cost hadn't started to mount. At school, I'd sneak off with my mates to the park for a smoke, and have a laugh with them. It felt like a club, and I felt good about belonging. Even then, I figured I could pack it in whenever I liked."

THE CHALLENGE

"Around the same time, I started going out with Kelly. I'd fancied her for ages and couldn't believe it when I heard she was interested in me. We went to the cinema for our first date. It was a long film, so I packed away two quick ciggies before we went in. I also lit up as soon as it finished, but because Kelly didn't smoke she drew attention to my habit."

Tic! Tic! Tic!

'Can't you go without a cigarette for more than a couple of hours?' she asked.
'Course!'
I protested.
'Prove it then',
she said.

WAKE UP CALL

"For the rest of our date I didn't touch the pack in my pocket. I was determined to prove that smoking was something I chose to do. At the same time, I realised how hard it was to go without. All I could think about was lighting up. Which I did. As soon as Kelly went home. The next day she asked me if I'd been tempted. I said I hadn't, but I'm sure she could tell I was lying. It was then I began to realise that I was hiding the truth from myself too. She was right, I'd found it hard to go without. It was then that I decided it was time to stop."

QUIT FOR GOOD?

"It's been months since I last smoked a cigarette, but even now I find it hard to avoid the temptation. Without a doubt, there's something really attractive about the ritual of lighting up. As soon as you fall into the habit, you wonder how you'll ever manage without again. Quitting takes guts, but the buzz from succeeding is unbeatable."

BURNING FACT:

Smoking is the number one cause of preventable deaths in the UK. More than 120,000 people die each year from smoke-related diseases. That's the equivalent of a jumbo jet full of passengers crashing every day.

CHAPTER TWO

The Damage

"You only have to look at my dad to see that he's a smoker. His fingers and teeth are stained yellow, and when he coughs it sounds like his lungs are totally filled with mush."

Annie, 14

"Smoking has certainly affected my sports performance. On the football pitch, my chest tightens up just minutes after kick off."

Neil, 16

"Sometimes I see pregnant women smoking a fag, and it makes me mad. I know it's none of my business, but I can't help thinking of that poor unborn baby having to deal with its mother's disgusting habit. As far as I'm concerned, it's like drink driving. Totally irresponsible!"

Rachel, 15

WHAT'S INSIDE A CIGGIE?

The shredded brown stuff inside a cigarette is called tobacco. This is basically a leaf which has been harvested from a tobacco plant then dried and processed. The final product actually contains about 4000 chemicals, many of which are harmful to your health. Cigarette tobacco includes stuff like formaldehyde, used for pickling things in jars; acetone, which is also found in nail varnish; ammonia, used in fertiliser and hydrogen sulphide, the odour you get from rotten eggs!

"I'm a smoker, but the smell of other people's cigarettes is enough to make me feel sick."

Rudi, 14

Taking a puff on a lit cigarette draws the smoke into the lungs. If the cigarette is filter tipped, then some of the chemicals are trapped as the smoke passes through, but not all. The end result is then inhaled into the lungs, absorbed into the bloodstream, and hits the brain about eight seconds later.

Of all the stuff crammed into a cigarette, the three biggest components are nicotine, carbon monoxide and tar.

Nicotine

The damage to health may be caused by the tar and poisonous chemicals, but it's the nicotine in tobacco which smokers can grow dependant upon.

"I get through about 10 a day, and more during the school holidays. I know I'm hooked because if I run out of smokes and I've got no cash then I panic."

Marcus, 16

Nicotine is a powerful and fast-acting stimulant drug. In small doses, it speeds up heart rate and increases blood pressure. This makes smokers feel more alert when they light up, while the brain activates a 'reward' system which is thought to be responsible for the pleasurable 'hit' they describe. Curiously enough, this 'happy hit' is very similar to the one triggered during sex!

The effect on an individual smoker depends on a number of different factors:

- Their physical build and current state of health.
- How long they have been smoking.
- How frequently they smoke.
- The number of puffs they take, and how deeply they inhale.

Tar

Cigarette smoke condenses when it's inhaled. This is a bit like watching droplets form upon the ceiling above a boiling kettle. The end result with smoking, however, is a whole lot more black and sticky. In fact about 70% of the tar present in tobacco smoke gets dumped into the lungs. It contains many substances which have been linked with cancer, as well as irritants that cause the narrow airways inside the lungs to get inflamed and clogged up with mucus.

"My granddad was a smoker, and when he died it took four months for the smell of stale cigarettes to leave his flat. My dad even had to repaint the sitting room because the walls were so discoloured."

Bridget, 15

Carbon monoxide

If you were to sort out a hit list of the most dangerous substances found in tobacco smoke, carbon monoxide would be public enemy number one. Carbon monoxide is a poisonous gas found in high concentration in cigarette smoke, not to mention the stuff which coughs out of car exhaust pipes. Once inside the lungs, the carbon atoms grab any passing haemoglobin, the oxygen forming substance found in the blood, and basically take a joy-ride around the body causing havoc in their wake.

"Just before my exams, I smoked so much it gave me a headache."

Michele, 15

Someone who smokes 20 a day can end up with a carbon monoxide level which is 5–10 times higher than that of a non-smoker. This deprives the blood of oxygen and makes it sticky, which can cause problems with growth, repair and exchange of healthy nutrients. In particular, any reduction in oxygen levels presents a real hazard to unborn babies. Pregnant women who smoke run a serious risk of miscarrying or having babies with low birth weight.

What's more, carbon monoxide can mess up electrical activity in the heart and encourage fatty deposits to clog up artery walls.

BURNING FACT: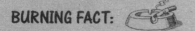

Someone who smokes 20 cigarettes a day takes 73,000 shots of nicotine into their brain cells each year.

THE DANGER ZONES

E veryone knows cigarettes are harmful to health, but it's easy to think the risks are much lower than they actually are. The fact is every cigarette you smoke can have a harmful effect on your body. It's effectively a nicotine injection. Giving up might put a halt to the harm, but it won't reverse the damage done. So the sooner you give up, the better. Should you carry on with the habit, here are some of the bits of your body which can suffer most:

Your lungs

The human lung is designed to extract oxygen from the air we breathe. It was never built to handle tobacco smoke. So every time a smoker inhales on a ciggie, their lungs take emergency action.

"The first time I took a drag on a cigarette, I virtually coughed my lungs up!"

Anna, 15

From the wind pipe down, the air you inhale passes into a network of passage ways called the bronchi. These divide into increasingly smaller branches called bronchioles, which finally end up in tiny air sacs called alveoli. It's here that blood vessels collect oxygen and distribute it around the body. When tar-heavy tobacco smoke floats into the mix, war breaks out inside the lungs, which can lead to some nasty medical conditions.

Bronchitis

The airways are lined by a carpet of tiny moving fronds. These wave about like seaweed in a current, and support a layer of sticky mucus. This serves to catch any dust or germs, before the whole snotty bundle works it back up into the throat, to be spat out or swallowed.

The irritants contained in tobacco smoke makes these fronds wilt, and can end up paralysing them completely. As a result, mucus hangs around for longer, becoming more and more bunged up with debris. Eventually, it has to be coughed up forcibly, leaving the airways red and raw. This is associated with airway infections and breathing problems such as bronchitis (or smoker's cough), which can become permanent.

"What's a smoker's cough? It's like a chesty cough only ten times worse, and which doesn't go away for ages. I know, because the guy next door smokes, and we sometimes hear him late at night, coughing up his guts"

Derry, 15

Emphysema

The lungs also contain an army of free-moving scavenger cells called phagocytes. They are basically the body's cleaners, hired to hoover up unwanted debris from lung tissue and keep things functioning normally. To do their job properly, phagocytes contain powerful chemicals to kill off germs and infection. Normally they are very careful about how much of this naturally-occuring cleaning fluid they use, because too much of the stuff can cause more harm than good. When cigarette smoke wafts over them, however, things get out of hand. Unwilling to put up with such lousy working conditions, the poor beseiged phagocytes show their annoyance by offloading their chemicals. As a result, vital lung tissue gets burned away. Never to be replaced.

This process is responsible for a disease called Emphysema. It kicks in pretty much as soon as you start smoking, but as you only use a small proportion of your lungs to breathe you may not notice any problems until it's too late. Emphysema can kill.

"My granddad smoked until the day he died, and it was obvious that his habit killed him. The last time I saw him, he was lying on his side in a hospice bed, wheezing so badly he could barely speak. Throughout my visit, he was constantly coughing up phlegm into a bowl. I was horrified. It sounded like his lungs had rotted."

Joe 15

A smoker's lungs contain nearly twice the amount of phagocytes than those of a non-smoker. With a heavier coating of tissue-killing chemicals, smoking transforms this vital organ into a battlefield. One which gets slowly destroyed as the fighting continues. Quitting will enable the lung's defence mechanism to stand at ease again, but it won't reverse the damage already done.

"I used to hold the school athletics record for the 800 metres. Then I started smoking, and within six months my time slipped so badly I lost my place in the squad."

David, 16

BURNING FACT:

Take 1,000 young smokers with a 20-a-day habit. On average, one will be murdered, six will die in road accidents, and 333 will die from smoking-related illness.

Your circulatory system

If the lungs are the front-line in the battle against the effects of smoking, the heart is the command centre. As soon as the enemy takes it out, you're dead. Literally. Here's how the effects of smoking works its way towards your ticker:

Blood clots and amputation

Once tobacco smoke has been broken down in the lungs, the chemical components are absorbed into the blood stream and quickly delivered all round the body. On the way, however, the very presence of such foreign bodies has a damaging effect on the blood itself. Not only does it mean space gets taken up that is otherwise reserved for oxygen, the red stuff also becomes thicker and harder to pump. What's more, certain cigarette smoke chemicals actually attack blood vessel walls.

As a result, smokers end up with a circulatory system that's overworked and weakened from the inside out. Bursts can occur. So too can blockages. Parts of the system can even shut down completely. The pay off for puffing away? Anything from fatal blood clots, to gangrene resulting in amputation of the toes, feet or limbs.

"My mum's a nurse. One day she took my sister and I into the ward, and introduced us to this guy in his 40's who'd just had his leg amputated at the thigh. He told us how smoking had been responsible for his lost limb, and then asked if I could wheel him outside for a fag!"

Nicky, 16

Heart attack

The heart itself is a sitting duck when it comes to the effects of smoking. All the blood in your body passes through it, and pools there between beats so all the oxygen can be sucked out. As nicotine in blood makes the heart beat faster, as well as causing vessels to tighten up, smokers run a real risk of a heart muscle being deprived of oxygen. Unable to function properly, the muscle panics by going into spasm that may well spark off a full blown heart attack.

"My uncle used to smoke, until he was diagnosed with angina. Basically he was getting chest pains, which is a sign that some of his heart muscles are in trouble. As a result he's been forced to change his lifestyle dramatically. Nowadays, he has to watch his diet, exercise very carefully, and take loads of pills. It's a scary way to live, knowing that your heart is close to packing up."

Helen, 15

BURNING FACT:

In the western world, 80% of all heart attacks in men under the age of 45 are due to smoking.

The threat of cancer

Before smoking became big business, lung cancer was a relatively rare disease. Today, it is the biggest cancer killer in the UK. The latest figures from the Imperial Cancer Research Fund estimate that more than 40,000 new cases occur each year.

Cigarette smoke is carcinogenic. This means anything it touches can increase the risk of cancer occuring. As a result, the damage doesn't stop in the lungs. Smoking has been linked to cancer of the mouth, nose, throat, pancreas, bladder and kidneys. Women who smoke are four times more likely to get cervical cancer, while the risk of contracting leukaemia (cancer of the blood) is greatly increased for anyone who ever lights up.

"When you bunk off for a smoke with your mates, the last thing you want to talk about is the effect on your health. I guess you just block it out. You don't want to think that the smoke you're pulling into your lungs might end up killing you."

Jane, 15

Getting your head around the risks is simple:
- The younger people start smoking, the greater the danger to their health.
- The more you smoke, the greater the risk you run of contracting a smoking-related illness such as bronchitis, emphysema or cancer.

Quitting is the best thing you can do for your body. As soon as you give up, the risks are vastly reduced.

● QUIZ ●

KEEP TABS ON YOUR HABIT

Reckon you could stop smoking just like that?
Here's four quit questions to find out for sure:

1 **It's time for your first cigarette of the day.
Do you:**
   a) *stop what you're doing and light up.*
   b) *finish what you're doing first.*
   c) *light up and then wish you'd waited.*

2 **You're at a party, but you've forgotten your
smokes. Would you:**
   a) *go out and buy a pack.*
   b) *cadge a few but smoke less than normal.*
   c) *stay smoke free. It's smoky enough as it is!*

3 **You plan to quit one hour from now.
Would you:**
   a) *tuck a few away to smoke when nobody's
      looking*
   b) *puff away nervously.*
   c) *prepare yourself by binning all lighters and
      ashtrays.*

4 **You've just given up, but going without is
making you moody. Do you:**
   a) *reach for a smoke. That's better!*

b) reach for the fridge. Chocolate?
   You deserve the whole bar!
c) reach for the phone. You need a mate to
   get your mind off things.

THE BOTTOM LINE:

If you answered:

Mostly _as_:
You're a hard-core smoker. Change your attitude
if you ever want to quit.

Mostly _bs_:
You're bordering on a habit which could easily get
a grip. Now's the time to think seriously about
packing it in.

Mostly _cs_:
You could stop if you really wanted. Set up a
plan and stick to it.

BURNING FACT:

In the UK, smoking kills one person every four and
half minutes.

CHAPTER THREE

Other Risks

Anti-smoking campaigns always push the message that cigarettes kill. But what really made me think about quitting was the fact that smokers get wrinkles earlier."

Toni, 15

"Smoking makes your breath stink."

Barry, 13

"Did you know that if a guy smokes a couple of ciggies it reduces the blood supply to his willy! My boyfriend smokes, but when I told him this he failed to see the funny side. Lads, eh? So touchy!"

Felicity, 15

Cancer? Lung disease? Heart attack? It's easy to ignore the long term health risks when you first get into smoking. Illnesses as serious as these seem light years away. Surely there's nothing to worry about for the time being, right? Wrong ...

Not only does every cigarette you smoke crank up your chances of dying from smoking-related illness, there are plenty more immediate worries too:

WRINKLY SKIN

Your skin is your body's protective suit. It's designed to shield you from the outside elements: heat, cold, wind, dirt and germs. Take your face, for example. It's an area more exposed than others, and it's also the first thing people are drawn to look at when they meet you. So it's understandable that we place loads of importance on keeping it looking good.

Each year, in the UK, we shell out over £4 billion pounds on stuff designed to care for the skin, from soaps to scrubs and moisturisers. If you smoke, however, then you're wasting your money. Because the real damage is happening from the inside out ...

To stay supple, your skin relies on a healthy blood supply. Nicotine constricts the vessels going into the skin, starving it of vital oxygen. On top of all this, toxins from cigarette smoke such as lead, ammonia and arsenic get delivered directly into the skin structure.

Every time you light up a smoke, you're effectively poisoning your skin. Sadly, it doesn't tolerate much before it starts to give up the ghost. It can't retain moisture so well, and wrinkles begin to develop. Slapping on the moisturiser won't make them go away. By then it's too late. You don't need to light up for people to know that you're a smoker. They can see it in your face.

"Six months ago, I started to get bad acne on my neck and forehead. My doctor explained that I had dry skin which was stimulating too much oil. She prescribed a cream which improved things a bit, but it wasn't until I quit smoking that my skin really cleared up."

Claire, 16

BURNING FACT:

Psoriasis is a medical condition that leaves the skin looking red, raw and scaly. 1 in 4 cases are thought to have been triggered by smoking.

SMOKER'S BREATH

Even if a smoker hasn't had a ciggie in hours, their breath can still smell bad. Basically, tobacco smoke dries out the membranes inside the mouth which are responsible for producing bacteria-beating saliva. As a result, all manner of bugs quickly start to fester and make their presence known. If you're the smoker, however, it's hard to know when your own breath smells. Reaching for the mouthwash might be a temporary solution, but it only takes another cigarette or two before people inch away from you whenever you start talking.

"My boyfriend always smokes a crafty fag on the way round to my house. The trouble is as soon as he steps inside he leaves this trail of stinky breath behind. I'm always telling him what a turn off it is, but he just claims I'm making it up. Sometimes I think smoking must shut down your sense of smell, because even the kitchen bin doesn't smell that bad!"

Bethan, 16

First impressions often count for everything. You may not have a ciggie in your hand at the time, but the people you're trying to impress will know what you've just been doing.

"I used to get annoyed when my mates kicked up a fuss about my breath every time I finished a smoke. It was only after I quit, and noticed the smell on other smokers, that I realised they weren't joking!"

Gary, 15

BURNING FACT:

More than 80% of all adult smokers started in their teens.

GUM PROBLEMS

Your teeth are held in place by your gums. It doesn't matter how strong your teeth may be, as soon as your gums start to go you'll be on soft foods in no time. Studies show that smoking is a major risk factor for the development and progression of periodontal gum disease. Basically, the mouth's defence mechanisms are crippled by exposure to regular blasts of tobacco smoke, which allows this gum-eating condition to run riot.

"My stepdad's a dentist, and he reckons that the young patients he sees who also happen to be smokers have the most problems with their gums. As far as he's concerned, smoking ages the contents of your gob!"

Alvin, 14

What's more, regularly smoking tobacco stains teeth yellow. Filters on cigarettes may cut down some of the effects, but often the worst affected areas are those you don't see at first glance:

"Everyone always says that smoking makes your teeth go bad, but I didn't see any change in mine until I visited the dentist. There, I got the shock of my life when I was told that it's the back of your teeth that come into greater contact with the smoke when you exhale. According to the dentist, mine were so stained they looked as if they'd gone rusty!"

Kedi, 16

BURNING FACT:

450 children start smoking every day in the UK.

SMOKING AND SEX

Cigarettes don't just damage your health, they can mess up your love life too! While smokers might be tempted to spark up after sex, chances are their performance in between the sheets could be vastly improved if they quit the habit completely. Here's how:

Erection problems

Guys, if you smoke then be aware that tobacco can seriously affect your todger. A growing wave of scientific evidence has shown that men who smoke are more likely to suffer from impotence (problems in getting or keeping an erection during sex).

Why? Because a healthy flow of blood is required through the penis in order to inflate it and keep things firm. For an erection to stay up, the inflow of blood through the arteries has to be greater than the outflow. Things get disappointing for smokers, however, when the inflow is restricted because nicotine has damaged artery walls. In some cases, puffing away on a couple of cigarettes before you slip between the sheets can completely stub out your chances of standing to attention!

"I enjoy smoking, but I don't like it so much that I'm prepared to let it mess with my tackle!"

Ramon, 15

BURNING FACT:

Smoking two high tar cigarettes in a short period of time reduces blood flow through the penis by a third. Keep up the habit and you could be letting yourself down badly. Recent studies suggest that up to 120,000 UK men have already made themselves impotent through smoking.

Fertility problems

Okay, so the prospect of having kids right now may be so far away you can't even see the horizon, but you should be aware that smoking now can badly compromise your chances of becoming a parent later on.

Nicotine can have a damaging effect on sperm quality and quantity. This means guys who smoke run the risk of turning the little fellas from a flotilla of natural-born swimmers to a trickle of slow-lane stragglers. In women, it's the ovaries which suffer by absorbing many of the toxic components of cigarette smoke.

Smoking can also increase the chances of an ectopic pregnancy (where the embryo is implanted outside the womb).

"My sister's 25 and has just started fertility treatment. One of the first things she was instructed to do was to persuade her husband to give up smoking!"

Mala, 15

"Smoking after sex sounds like one of the most unromantic things two people can do."

Lloyd, 16

BURNING FACT:

Breast-fed babies whose mothers smoke are exposed to nicotine through their milk, often up to half a cigarette's worth a day.

Smoking and the contraceptive pill

The female oral contraceptive pill contains low doses of certain hormones that prevent users from getting pregnant. This is a perfectly safe form of birth control. However, women who use the pill are advised not to smoke. This is because the chemicals from tobacco messes around with blood composition, and when combined with the effects of the pill can increase the chance of blood clots and heart disease.

"My doctor agreed to prescribe the pill on condition that I quit smoking. The way he explained things, I'd be doing my physical health a big favour, as well as looking after my sexual health."

Lisa, 16

BURNING FACT:

Recent research suggests that people who smoke are over 50% more likely than non-smokers to have serious relationship problems, including a greater likelihood of suffering from anxiety and depression.

SMOKING AND THE LAW

It may not be illegal to smoke at any age, but you run a big risk if you're under 16:

- The police can take away cigarettes from anyone under 16 who is seen to be smoking in a public place.
- It's illegal for a shop keeper to sell cigarettes to anyone under 16, even if they are for someone else. The same rule applies to other smoking bits and pieces like cigars, cigarette papers and rolling tobacco.

"Once I got stopped by the police for smoking in the park. They gave me a really heavy lecture, and I was terrified my parents would find out - especially because a load of people from my street stopped to gawp!"

Jonathan, 14

BURNING FACT: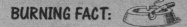

50% of all regular long-term smokers will be killed by their habit.

THE COST OF SMOKING

Apart from the risk to your health, a smoking habit can have a serious effect on your cash situation too. Cigarettes don't come cheap, and for some this can be a big incentive to quit. Here's what smoking ten cigarettes a day could cost you:

After:

one week:	A full-price CD
one month:	A new outfit
six months:	A return flight to the USA
12 months:	A new hi-fi, TV and video player

When you stop to do the sums, smoking just doesn't work out.

"As soon as I quit I noticed my pockets started filling up! It's not until you actually give up that you appreciate how much money you burn on cigarettes."

Rab, 16

BURNING FACT: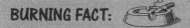

In one decade, a 20-a-day smoker will blow around 20, 000 pounds on cigarettes.

REAL LIFE

L ana, 15, thought she'd kept her smoking habit a secret from her parents. Then a passing comment from her dad made her think again:

"My mum and dad have never touched a single cigarette in their lives. When I was a kid they used to drum the message home that smoking was bad, and could even kill. As a result, I just couldn't understand why people chose to smoke. So when I was 14 and a couple of my mates got into the habit I was fascinated to find out why."

EARLY EXPERIMENTS

"My first puff on a cigarette was also my last, but only for about a month. It was a disgusting experience and I understood what my parents meant when they said it was a foul habit. I never thought I would try it again. The problem was that more of my friends were lighting up. After school, or at the shopping mall, someone always had a pack of ciggies. Finally, I gave in, and sparked up just so I wouldn't feel left out. To begin I didn't even inhale. I just held the smoke in my mouth for a second before blowing it out. Then someone noticed, and once the laughter had died down I was shown how to do it properly."

HIDING THE HABIT

"The first time I bought my own cigarettes, I stashed them at a friend's house. I was so scared that my parents would find out that I didn't want to take any risks. After a while, however, I started to drop my guard and hide them in my bedroom. I even grabbed the chance to smoke in the garden whenever my folks went out. Not once did I stop to think that the tell-tale smell on my breath or my clothes might give me away."

MORE LIES

"Six months later, I was smoking 10 to 15 cigarettes a day. I had an allowance from my dad, and nothing more, so most of my cash went on fags. If I saw something in town that I really liked, such as a shirt or a CD, I'd pester my mum until she gave in and paid for it. I remember she'd always ask me where my money went, and I'd cobble together some story about blowing it on burgers and trips to the cinema (even though I rarely went). I always just assumed she believed me."

DISCOVERING THE TRUTH

"Everything went wrong after a party one Saturday evening, when my dad came to pick me up. As always, after I got in the car I opened the window immediately so he wouldn't smell tobacco on me. With fresh air whizzing around I figured I was safe. Then my dad just came right out and asked me:

'So how many did you smoke tonight?'

I was stunned. I felt sick and numb. In a panic, I said I didn't know what he was talking about.

'Funny that,' he said. 'I can't remember the last time you didn't smell of stale cigarettes.'

'It's my friends!' I protested. 'Everyone smokes but me. Honest!'

My dad just nodded, and we drove the rest of the way home in silence. That night, I hardly slept."

REGRET

"My dad knew I was lying, and I felt really lousy for even thinking he'd believe me. I should have come clean, I realised. He'd given me the chance to get things out in the open and all I could do was deny everything. Worse still, it seemed he'd known all along. As a result, I felt like I'd badly disappointed him. He never mentioned the episode again, but it made me think hard about what I was doing."

MAKING THE BREAK

"In just six months, I'd picked up a smoking habit and learned how to lie to my mum and dad. It wasn't much to be proud about. One day after our 'chat', I vowed to kick the habit. It took me a couple of goes, but I got there in the end. As for my dad, I think he knew what he was doing all along. He never once shouted at me, or made me feel bad. By playing it calm, he left me to learn from my own mistakes."

CHAPTER FOUR

Other Smokers

"I can't remember the last time I saw my dad without a roll-up sticking out of his mouth."

Jaz, 15

"Smoking has never appealed to me, even though my brother's been into the habit for years. Basically, I've seen what it's done to his health. Nowadays, whenever there's a cough or a cold doing the rounds, he's always the one who finds it hardest to shake off."

Christine, 14

"I wouldn't swap my girlfriend for the world, but I'd do anything for her to give up the cigarettes."

Geordie, 15

Even if you're a committed non-smoker, it's virtually impossible for a day to go by without catching a whiff of tobacco. Whether you happen to stand downwind from someone who flashes the ash at a bus stop, or a member of your family lights up all the time, smoking is an issue you can't afford to ignore.

PASSIVE SMOKING

When someone sparks up a fag not all the tobacco smoke produced heads straight for their lungs. The smoke you see coiling off the glowing ember drifts into the air, to be breathed in by anyone unlucky enough to be standing nearby.

This is known as passive smoking, and it can be more harmful than sucking directly on the ciggie itself. How? Because most cigarettes are fitted with filters, which absorb at least some of the toxins in tobacco smoke. Unlike the stinky stuff which curls off the lit end between drags. Combined with the smoke which is then exhaled from the lungs, the whole package is enough to make you choke.

"In school we once dissected a used cigarette butt. The inside of a filter looked like thick cotton wool, only it was stained brown from the smoke which had passed through."

Holden, 14

"If I go to a party where loads of people are smoking, I always come away with a sore throat."

Alice, 15

Ultimately, when someone lights up it's not just other people who are affected by passive smoking. Even the smoker has to breathe between drags!

BURNING FACT:

200 people die every year in the UK from a passive-smoking related disease.

The effects of passive smoking

Nowadays, most people accept that there are significant health risks associated with passive smoking. Worst affected are those who experience regular exposure over a long period of time, such as children who grow up in smoky homes. In fact, studies show that children of smokers are more likely to suffer health problems such as chest infections than those who live in a ciggie-free environment.

"Both my parents smoke. They try not to light up when I'm in the room, but that doesn't stop the whole house reeking."

Trent, 14

Not only do smokers increase their own risk of cancer and cardiovascular (heart) disease, it's thought they also increase the odds for those around them. Not just humans, but pets too!

"Our dog died of leukaemia last year. Although the vet couldn't say what had caused the disease, he asked if anyone in the family smoked. My dad, who smokes a pack a day, went very quiet."

Mikey, 15

BURNING FACT: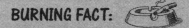

It is estimated that living with a smoker on a long-term basis increases your chances of dying from lung cancer by 26%.

Your right to clean air

Smokers can be very sensitive about lighting up in the company of non-smokers. Many will go to great lengths to avoid polluting the air for others. However, there's always someone who will spark up regardless of the nuisance and pollution it causes.

"I have a right to smoke. I know it's bad for my health, but it's my body and my life. I'll do what I want with it!"

Nick, 16

"I don't feel comfortable sparking up in a room with someone who doesn't smoke. Why should they have to put up with my habit?"

Amber, 15

In recent years, as people have become more aware of the dangers of passive smoking, non-smokers have demanded the right to breathe clean air. As a result, most public places have now established smoking policies. In some places, like cafes and restaurants, smoking is banned entirely, while others set aside certain areas for smoking.

"Across the road from our school there's an office with a no-smoking policy. Every time I glance through the window there's always someone in a suit puffing away on the step. Even in the driving rain!"

Hugh, 14

"Whenever I get on a train I avoid the smokers' compartment. It's always packed, and choked with smoke. Even though I'm usually desperate for a ciggie myself, I'd rather go without and get a seat."

Judy, 16

BURNING FACT: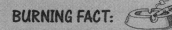

83% of the UK public would like to see an increase in no-smoking areas.

DEALING WITH SMOKERS

Smoking in public might be subject to rules and regulations but closer to home things are often not so clear cut. Perhaps someone in your family smokes. Maybe some of your mates have got into the habit, or even the person you're dating. If you're a non-smoker, and you don't fancy breathing polluted air, then you need to make your opinions known. It's just a question of knowing how to handle each situation.

Dealing with parents

Parents always know best. At least that's what most of us are raised to be believe. Our folks are there to guide us, and lead by example. So when your dad breaks off the lecture to spark up a ciggie, it's easy to think you have no right to point out the error of his ways.

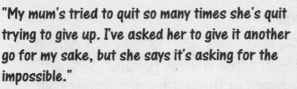

"Even though my parents smoke, they'd go bananas with me if I ever took up the habit."

Ella, 14

"My mum's tried to quit so many times she's quit trying to give up. I've asked her to give it another go for my sake, but she says it's asking for the impossible."

Miles, 15

If one of your folks smokes, and it's getting up your nose, then take a deep breath and follow these wise words:

AVOID CONFRONTATION

Nobody likes feeling under attack, or being made to feel they're in the wrong. Smokers, in particular, can become very defensive when someone has a go at them about their habit. So avoid steaming in, stubbing out their ciggie, and accusing of them passive poisoning. It'll only end up in a row. Ultimately, you can't force a smoker to give up. The commitment to quit has to come from them.

RESPECT

No smoker deliberately sets out to annoy other people. They smoke because they enjoy the habit, or they feel unable to go without. Make your parent aware of the fact that you understand their situation, and you're more likely to get a positive response.

NEGOTIATE

Next, you need to flag up how their habit affects you. Arm them with the facts about passive smoking. Let them know you're concerned, and make sure you listen to what they have to say.

COMPROMISE

If your parent refuses to quit, or tries but fails, then seek to establish some middle ground. Set up no-smoking zones in the house, or suggest that they step outside whenever they feel the need for a nicotine fix. Even if you stand on opposite sides of the smoking argument, be big about it and meet half way.

Dealing with brother and sisters

When people first light up, they tend to hide the habit from their parents. If you've discovered that your brother or sister is a secret smoker, then you could find yourself in a difficult situation.

"My mum would go mad if she found out my brother smokes. I hate lying to her, but he made me swear I wouldn't say anything."

Martha, 13

"Sometimes my sister asks me to say she's gone to the shops when in fact she's nipped out for a ciggie."

Julian, 15

The trouble with keeping quiet about a sibling's smoking habit is that you risk getting sucked into trouble when they get found out.

Here's what to do if you're unhappy about covering up for them:

• DON'T BE PRESSURED

If your brother or sister want to smoke, they must take responsibility for their actions. Not you. Threatening to blab to your parents will only cause tension, as will trying to use their secret as a bargaining chip for future favours.

• BE HONEST

Let them know where you stand on the issue, and be clear about how you'll respond if a parent gets suspicious. If you're uneasy about lying then say so, just reassure them that you won't be broadcasting the news unprompted. They'll have to respect your decision.

• GIVE THEM THE FACTS

If you're concerned for their health, highlight the risks involved and let them make up their own minds.

• BE SUPPORTIVE

Let them know that you're prepared to help if they want to quit.

Dealing with friends

Mates who smoke often assume you won't mind if they light up around you. You're one of them, they think. Not a figure of authority, like a parent or teacher. As a result, you find yourself putting up with their habit because you don't want to seem like a killjoy.

"If I'm round at my friend's house, and his mum goes out, he always expects me to stand outside with him while he smokes himself stupid."

Davíd, 15

"During a party at my house recently, a couple of mates started smoking without asking. I felt really bad about getting them to stop, but they were taking liberties and my parents would have flipped."

Penny, 14

If you're out with a mate, but you're choking on their smoke, here's how to sort it out and stay the friends:

• STAND PROUD AS A NON-SMOKER

There's no shame in steering clear of cigarettes. The whole idea that smoking somehow makes you a cooler, more attractive person is an outdated myth. So don't suffer their habit in silence, or be made to feel like you're out of touch for claiming your right to clean air.

• PUT YOUR FRIENDSHIP BEFORE THE PACK

When a group of friends get into smoking, it's easy for a clique to form. This clique can sometimes seem closed off to anyone who doesn't smoke, but don't let it break up a friendship. If a mate's putting their habit before you then discuss the issue with them before it gets out of hand.

• RESIST THE TEMPTATION TO PREACH

Respect plays a central role in any friendship. You may not like the fact that your mate lights up like it's going out of fashion, but criticising will only cause a rift between you. If you want to help, don't preach. Just give them the facts about smoking, and let them make up their own minds. Even if they don't quit, they should at least keep their habit out of your face.

Smoking in a romance

All couples have their differences. You may share a great deal in common but ultimately you're both individuals. Sometimes issues crop up that divide you. Flouncing isn't the answer. A strop never solved anything. The secret to a stress-free romance is knowing how to talk things through.

"I wish my girlfriend didn't smoke. I've tried to persuade her to pack it in but she just gets cross and says she doesn't need to be told."

Brian, 14

"My boyfriend gets really twitchy whenever he runs out of cigarettes. It doesn't matter if we're snuggled up in front of the video, he has to go and buy some more."

Rona, 15

If you're dating a smoker, here's how to stop the cigarettes from coming between you:

• DISCUSS THE ISSUE

If smoking is an issue in your relationship, don't bottle up your feelings about it. Staying quiet won't solve the problem. Instead you're more likely to seethe about it to yourself, and could even end up resenting them whenever they light up. To avoid a scene, let them know how you feel about smoking right from the start. But be prepared to listen, too. Chances are they won't quit on the spot, but your gentle reminder that there is life without cigarettes will at least get them thinking.

• SHOW RESPECT

So you're dating a smoker. Even if their habit really gets up your nose, don't lose sight of all the reasons why you were attracted to them in the first place. Ultimately, their nicotine habit is just one small thorn in a bed of roses. Don't throw away your whole relationship for the sake of a lousy ciggie!

• BE REASONABLE

If you're involved with someone who refuses to quit, it's important not to take it personally. Claiming they'd give up if they really loved you won't help the situation, and nor would it be true. People give up smoking when they feel ready and able to do so. Not when they're told.

• WORK TOGETHER

Sometimes, couples find they can't agree on something no matter how hard they try. But this doesn't mean they have to break up. It means they have to negotiate a compromise. One that works for both sides. Don't let smoking stub out a relationship. Just keep offering your support should they finally decide to quit.

BURNING FACT:

50% of 11-15 year olds who smoke say they'd find it hard to go a day without a cigarette.

SMOKING STRIFE

Question
"A mate of mine saw my little brother smoking on the way home from school. I confronted him about it, but he denied everything. Mum would hit the roof if she found out, so is there anything else I can do?"

Lindsey, 15

Answer:
If your brother's started smoking, it's his responsibility. Telling your mum at this stage will only turn him against you. If you want to be an influence in getting him to give up, then stay on his side. To do so, you need to take a different approach.

This time, don't throw accusations at him. It'll only put him on the defensive. If you want an honest answer then make him aware that you understand the facts about smoking, and that you're only concerned because of the risks involved. Not just to his health, but to his well being should your mum find out!

Try not to make him feel guilty or threaten to blab if he doesn't give up. Just ask him to think about quitting. You can't force him to stub out the habit, but you can be there to help when he's ready.

Question:

"My dad's a smoker and I really want him to quit. I've tried telling him he's killing us all, but he just gets up tight and says he'll give up in his own time."

Alex, 13

Answer:

While it's great that you're concerned about your dad's nicotine habit, try not to put too much pressure on him. A smoker who's preparing to break free needs support. Nagging them just leads to tension.

Instead, just hand him the facts about smoking, including the risks of passive smoking, and leave it at that. If he really wants to quit, he'll do it.

Question:

"I told my boyfriend that I'd finish with him if he didn't quit smoking. To my surprise he made no effort to pack in the habit, and I didn't feel able to back down. Is it too late to make up with him?"

Harriet, 14

Answer:

While it's clear you had your boyfriend's health interests at heart, you went the wrong way about getting him to wise up.

When it comes to giving up smoking, threats and ultimatums rarely work. If a smoker's not ready to stop, it often just reinforces their commitment to the habit.

If you genuinely regret walking out on this guy, then talk to him about it. Just keep an open mind, not just about reviving the romance but about his smoking too. You may have failed to persuade him to quit this time, but chances are you started the clock ticking towards the day he makes the break!

BURNING FACT:

Someone living in a smoky home environment inhales the equivalent of two cigarettes a week.

CHAPTER FIVE

Dealing with Temptation

"Everyone knows smoking is addictive, but when you first get into the habit you think you'll be able to stop before you get hooked."

Gail, 14

"I thought that if I just smoked at parties I wouldn't get addicted. Now I wish I'd never started at all!"

Marcus, 15

"At 13, I was badly tempted to start smoking. I only held out because I was worried about my folks finding out. As I got older, however, my reasons changed. Basically, I became more aware of the risks involved. It meant that instead of being scared about getting into trouble, I was more concerned for the effect on my appearance! I'm 16 now, and when I watch my mates struggling to quit I look back and realise that the longer you steer clear of cigarettes the easier it is to deal with the temptation."

Tanya, 16

If you haven't been tempted to try a cigarette, you will soon. Chances are you know someone who smokes, and it won't be long before you'll be invited to join them. But choosing whether to light up or leave it doesn't just depend on how much you understand about the risks. Ultimately, if you want to make a decision you can live with, you have to understand yourself and why you're being seduced. That way, it's not so hard to speak your mind when someone waves that first ciggie in your face.

WHAT IS TEMPTATION?

The dictionary defines temptation as the desire to do something, especially something wrong and unwise. We all know smoking kills, but in some ways this is at the heart of the attraction. None of us want to die early on our journey through life, but things always seems so much more exciting in the fast lane. It might be a buzz, but not only do you increase your chances of crashing, you're also going to reach your destination before everyone else. So who's in a hurry now?

"I tried my first cigarette because I wanted to. Nobody forced me, but I didn't exactly think hard about it. At the time, you forget about the risks and just go for it."

Warren, 14

BURNING FACT:

You're four times more likely to try a cigarette if you have a brother or sister who smoke. Resist it.

WHY AM I TEMPTED?

People decide to try their first cigarette for different reasons. Here are some of the guiding influences:

- **Peer pressure:** When everyone else is lighting up it's easy to feel left out. Even if the habit doesn't appeal, being a non-smoker can leave you feeling excluded from the circle.
- **Curiosity:** We know smoking is something that won't do us any favours, but our mates seem to enjoy it so why shouldn't we?
- **Impulse:** When it comes to the crunch, most people accept their first cigarette on the spur of the moment. There's rarely any forward planning involved. Just a snap decision to see what all the fuss is about.

"At break time, my mates always nip off for a smoke. I only go with them because I don't want to hang around on my own."

Keo, 14

"I guess the fact that my dad kept warning me not to smoke was part of the reason why I tried it! After all, no-one likes to be told what to do!"

Sylvia, 15

BURNING FACT:

The younger you start, the more likely you are to get hooked. Regular smokers are much more likely than occasional smokers to have had their first cigarette before the age of 11.

Tobacco advertising: the big sell out

It's not just peer pressure, or the lure of the taboo, that appeals to the potential smoker. The image sold to us by the tobacco manufacturing giants also plays a role. One that is as subtle as it is powerful.

"When you see a racing car roar around the circuit, and it's plastered with tobacco sponsorship, you can't help but think it's a pretty cool brand."

Jon, 14

Complex health regulations govern cigarette advertising. In fact, just recently new laws were introduced into the UK banning ads on billboards and in magazines. Even so, it's safe to say that tobacco-branding won't disappear altogether. Many sports and arts events still have a few years left before tobacco sponsorship is outlawed, while it's likely that the baccy industry will simply move on to target stuff like clothing, holidays, clubs and even coffee shops. So if cigarette branding refuses to vanish in a puff of smoke, it's important to recognise what's being pushed in your face.

Wherever they get to stick their ads and trade names, tobacco manufacturers are legally restricted about the claims they can make. As a result, cigarette branding and imagery often says very little about the product, and aims instead to sell you a lifestyle. The idea is that you take one look at some trendy back pack emblazoned with the name of a cigarette company, and immediately light up in a bid to kindle a sense of adventure, independence and freedom!

It's unlikely that anyone would take such a message on board so dramatically. Even so, the constant presence of such glamorous ciggie-related imagery can be very attractive. Especially at a time when you're busy working out who you are, and what kind of self-image you want to build. Whether you're male or female, there's something in the way we're sold cigarettes that's designed to appeal to the potential smoker in us all.

 "You can't deny that cigarette cartons are made to look cool. Either they're super-streamlined and sporty, or embossed with gold and made to look like you're loaded!"
Petra, 16

Cigarette imagery may not be directly responsible for kick starting someone into smoking, but its influence is undeniable. Just think how many times you're encouraged to think about smoking in a positive light. Not just on trendy T-shirts or at sports events, but by association with celebs. A star photographed with a fag in their hand is a tobacco manufacturer's dream. Especially if they're dumb enough to have the carton on view too! No amount of money could pay for the kind of message this conveys. It says 'here's someone who's succeeded and smokes!' Its just a shame no-one wants to see pics of the same celeb years later, wheezing into an oxygen mask while a nurse wheels them around the hospital grounds.

Whatever it takes, tobacco manufacturers are committed to making their product a familiar and friendly name. Why? Because if they want to protect their massive profits then it's vital that they recruit 330 new smokers every 24 hours. For that's the number of customers they lose each day to smoking-related deaths.

So next time you see some kind of fancy cigarette imagery, think of the motive behind the message. No matter how cool, witty or sophisticated it might appear, be smart and don't get sucked in.

BURNING FACT: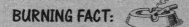

In a recent survey, half of all 16-24 year olds felt that tobacco sponsorship of sporting events should be banned.

RESISTING TEMPTATION

So you're sussed about the risks. You know that smoking kills, and can mess up your body from the very first puff. You also understand why the habit has such a seductive image, and who benefits from all the cash you shell out. And yet despite it all, the temptation to spark up can still be as powerful as ever.

"It was easier to just take one cigarette and try it, than to say no and have people thinking I was Mrs Square."

Nell, 14

Nobody sets out to get hooked on smoking on purpose. If you knew that first experimental puff was going to spark a lifelong habit that could eventually kill, then chances are you'd pass. Wouldn't you?

Sadly, it's all too easy to think an addiction is something that happens to other people. By the time you get real, it's often too late. So here's how to beat the different stages of temptation before it becomes a vice:

Thanks, but no thanks . . .

It's natural to want to belong, and feel like part of a group. But before you go ahead and give in, ask yourself whether sticking a ciggie in your gob is really going to make you any more popular and attractive. Will your mates really think any less of you if you decide to pass this time?

"Only one of my mates doesn't smoke. He's never hesitated in turning down the offer of a cigarette, and I respect him for that. As far as I'm concerned, he's got more sense of identity than the rest of us put together!"
Tim, 16

BURNING FACT:

In a UK survey of teen smoking habits, 81% of eleven year olds had never smoked. Four years later, only 30% could say they had never tried it.

Just one more . . .

Nobody enjoys their first pull on a ciggie. It leaves you coughing all over the place while your mates look on and laugh. Unfortunately, your belief that such a disgusting experience can possibly be addictive also goes up in smoke.

"The first cigarette tastes so disgusting that you can't think how anyone could get hooked. So you try another, because you think you can get away with it . . ."

Pedro, 13

BURNING FACT:

Smokers chuck away 300 million cigarette butts every day in the UK.

Me? A smoker? Never!

Maybe you've choked your way through a whole cigarette and survived. It didn't seem so bad, you think. But it's not something you'd do on a regular basis. Maybe just at parties. Simply to fit in. That doesn't make you a smoker, does it?

"I always used to think of myself as a casual smoker. Something I did at weekends. Then I went on holiday for a fortnight with my parents, where I found I couldn't relax until I sneaked off and bought a pack for myself."

Donald, 15

BURNING FACT: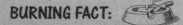

In the UK, smoking kills over 2000 people each week.

Quitting is easy

Even after you've woken up to the fact that you might have become a smoker, it takes a lot longer to accept that you can't easily give up. But then what's the rush? You're young, and quitting is big business nowadays. There are loads of different methods out there on the market. It can't be that difficult, can it?

"My first attempt at giving up lasted two hours. It was a real-wake up call for me, because I'd only been smoking for a couple of months. Within minutes of my last cigarette, I found myself panicking about whether I could go without. After I caved in, things were never the same. Every time I reached for a cigarette I just felt helpless. It's not a nice feeling."

Glyn, 15

BURNING FACT:

If your parents smoke, you are twice as likely to take up the habit. A family tradition they'll want you to break!

I'll give up tomorrow

Maybe you've got to the stage where you've tried to give up and failed. In this situation, it's tempting to think there's no point even attempting to quit. After all, it's easier reaching for a cigarette than it is looking for a reason to avoid one.

> "I lasted three days on my first attempt to give up. I was shocked by how hard it had been, and resigned myself to the fact that I was destined to be a smoker. I finally quit a year later, and it was only then that I realised I'd been kidding myself. I'd just been too frightened to face up to the addiction."
>
> Natalie, 15

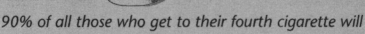

BURNING FACT:

90% of all those who get to their fourth cigarette will end up long-term smokers.

It's only money!

Everyone knows that smoking costs a lot of cash. Of course, it doesn't seem like a big deal every time you shell out a couple of quid, but over a period of time the habit will cost you dearly. Yet would you be so tempted if you knew exactly where that cash was going?

For every packet you buy:
- 7% goes to the retailer
- 15% goes to the tobacco manufacturer
- 78% goes to the government

In other words, the state, the ciggie maker and the shopkeeper are making a mint from you. Not only is more than two-thirds of your smoke going on taxes, the main manufacturers are profiting from your habit to the tune of hundreds of millions of pounds each year.

"Whenever I buy a packet of smokes I always feel as if I'm being ripped off."

Will, 16

BURNING FACT:

It is estimated that nearly a billion cigarettes are smoked by 11-15 year olds each year. From this, the government makes well over £100,000,000 in tax, even though it's illegal for this age group to be sold tobacco!

LOOKING BACK ON TEMPTATION

Whatever stage you're at in the smoking game, whether people around you have started lighting up, or you've just slipped into the habit, stop for a minute and ask whether you could walk away from it. Why not try the next time you're faced with a cigarette. The temptation might be powerful, but the moment never lasts long. What's more, you'll get a far bigger buzz from resisting it than you would from any nicotine hit.

"When I first started smoking, my best friend refused to even take a drag. I used to take the mickey out of him for being boring. Now I wish I'd followed his lead."

Stuart, 15

BURNING FACT: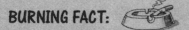

In a recent survey, 34% of boys claimed they tried their first cigarette before the age of 11, compared to 24% of girls.

TEN WAYS TO TRASH THE TEMPTATION

At a loss for words when someone offers you a ciggie? Here's 10 face-saving put-downs to stay smoke free:

1. You're asking the wrong person.
2. Why would I want to hide behind a smoke screen?
3. Not today! Not tomorrow! Not the day after!
4. No ta, I'm too addicted to fresh air.
5. Something in my heart says no.
6. No, I gave up smokers yonks ago.
7. Sorry, but I love my lungs.
8. I know my mind.
9. Sorry, but I need my hands free for hugging.
10. Butt out!

CHAPTER SIX

So You Want to Quit?

"I'd love to give up smoking, but I'm too scared to try in case I fail."

Kari, 15

"I can't imagine what it must be like to go a day without craving a cigarette."

Dexter, 14

"I know I'd feel better not smoking, and it would save me loads of money. But whenever I run out I always seem to find an excuse to buy another packet."

Rhys, 15

Sparking up is easy when everyone else is smoking. Giving up takes guts. It's one of life's most addictive habits. One which makes stopping such a great achievement.

The problem is quitting cigarettes isn't as simple as starting. For some, the whole prospect of going without can be unthinkable. But with the right motivation, bags of determination, and a tailor-made strategy, anyone can free themselves from the habit.

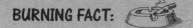

BURNING FACT:

In the UK, smokers chuck away 20 million cigarette packets a day. Why not bin the habit completely?

REASONS TO QUIT

Maybe you've been thinking about stopping for a while, or perhaps the idea's just come into your head. Either way, you've taken an important first step towards quitting. Now check out some of the rewards you get by going all the way:

Improved health

Things get better from the moment you stub out your final fag. As soon as you quit, your body basically throws open the windows and lets the fresh air in. After just 20 minutes, your blood pressure returns to normal levels. Within 24 hours, your lungs start to clear out the rubbish, while the final traces of carbon monoxide are rounded up and shown to the door. Think about it. Wouldn't it be good to spring-clean your system?

> "Before quitting I had no idea how much better I would feel. Now I wake up without a headache, and don't get that horrible tightness in my chest whenever I break into a run. When you're smoker, I guess you just put up with it."

> Howard, 15

BURNING FACT:

Statistics show that 69% of all smokers in the UK would like to quit. 83% of them stated health worries as the major reason.

More cash

Not only are you going to save a wedge of cash by giving up, another good motivation for making the break is to think about the money you've already spent on the habit. If you've been smoking five cigarettes a day for the last six months, for example, then you will have burned roughly £180! Ouch!

"When you've just given up, and you need a reason to continue, just count out the money you've saved by staying off the ciggies. It worked for me!"

Mark, 14

BURNING FACT:

46% of regular teenage smokers light up within an hour of waking. Some breakfast!

Less stink

Tobacco smoke clings to smokers. Even if you're not actually puffing away at the time, people can tell you're a slave to the habit. The smell infests everything from your clothes, to your hair and your breath. It's a stink that gets worse as it gets stale.

Often, smokers are so used to it that they don't even notice. Until they quit, and things suddenly start to smell much sweeter.

"My boyfriend really appreciated it when I packed in the smokes. I know, because he was suddenly much more enthusiastic about kissing me!"

Bonny, 13

BURNING FACT:

In Great Britain alone, it is estimated that there are more than 10 million people who have successfully given up smoking.

Taste and smell

Quit the cigs and the only food that'll taste a bit smoked is the stuff you sling on the barbie. *Everything* will taste better. Including you. As for your nostrils, it'll be like being born again. Very quickly, you'll realise just how much you missed for the sake of a nicotine hit.

BURNING FACT:

Smoking is known to worsen any allergies you may have, and can often trigger asthma attacks.

Sense of achievement

Everyone has different reasons for quitting, but all share the same sense of achievement. The knock-on effect from giving up smoking is huge. Knowing that you've cracked one of the hardest addictions going is enough to boost anyone's self-confidence. If you can quit the cigs, you can take on anything life throws at you.

"Just getting through the first day was a kick. It was enough to get me through the next, and so on. Eventually, you set your sights on weeks, then months. Hopefully even years."

Annalisa, 15

BURNING FACT:

Smoking could leave your skin up to 40% thinner, making early wrinkles likely. So give it up, and stay young!

PREPARING TO QUIT

Why now?

So you know why you want to quit, but are you determined to see it through? Some smokers know instinctively when the time is right. Others aren't so sure.

If something's holding you back, write down all the reasons why you started smoking, why you continue to smoke, and the reasons why you want to stop. Things may not become clearer straight away, but it'll challenge you to conquer your doubts and cross them off your list. Eventually, you'll be left with nothing but motivation - the key to successful quitting!

"I made two failed attempts at giving up before I finally cracked it. The third time, unlike before, I knew in my heart that I would do it."

Alan, 15

BURNING FACT:

The tobacco plant is a member of the Nightshade family, which includes the poisonous, Deadly Nightshade!

Says who?

Whatever your reasons for wanting to give up, the desire to stop has to come from you. Your friends and family may nag you about quitting, but it's down to you to make the decision. Ultimately, you have to want to quit, however you choose to go about it.

If you're feeling pressured into giving up you'll only resent making the break. To be sure that you're quitting for the right reasons, it's important that you admit you have a problem. Ask yourself whether you smoke out of personal choice, or because you feel you have no choice. If the latter rings alarm bells, then you're on the right road to packing it in.

"When my mum found out I smoked, she made me swear I'd stop. But it didn't work. I only quit when I decided enough was enough."

Millie, 15

BURNING FACT:

In a recent survey, 48% of women said they felt emotionally dependent on cigarettes, compared to 35% of men.

What for?

The prospect of quitting doesn't exactly fill anyone with joy. It can be hugely daunting, which is why you need to be clear about your reasons for giving up. Identify what it is you will achieve by breaking free from cigarettes, and make it central to your quitting campaign.

"I quit because I hated reaching for my cigarettes whenever I got stressed. It was something I felt I should be able to sort without sparking up. And I did!"

Anthea, 14

BURNING FACT:

When smokers first try to control their habit, men generally tend to cut down their cigarette intake, while women switch to lower tar brands. In both cases, however, smokers end up taking in more nicotine by inhaling harder to get the hit they crave. Whoops!

What if?

The prospect of quitting might make you nervous, but just think how much better you'll feel in two weeks time, or even a month. After that, you'll be measuring things in years! Fingers crossed you'll get that far, but at every stage it's important to have a reward lined up. A special treat to get you through. There may be tough times ahead, so make sure you set your sights on something that honours your achievement!

"My dad said that if I gave up for six months, he would match the money I saved by not smoking. I jumped at the chance, first because of the cash but later because I wanted to prove to him, and to myself, that I could do it."

Justin, 15

BURNING FACT: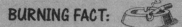

Quit smoking 10 cigarettes a day, save around £14 a week.

GO FOR IT!

Once you've set your sights on quitting, the next step is to establish your campaign. The trick is to be prepared for any situation or emotion you might experience. Think it through. Plan ahead. If you can consider every aspect of your day to day life where cigarettes normally feature, you'll be able to work out the most effective way to avoid the temptation.

"After smoking your final cigarette, the worst moment comes when you would normally light up the next. I only got through it by promising myself I could have the one after. Of course, when you get to that one you skip it and do the same thing again. After a day or so, things get less intense."

Irene, 15

"On the morning I quit I stocked up with fruit and vegetables. I ended up 'smoking' about four carrots before lunch-time, but I felt much better as a result!"

Erin, 16

YOUR QUITTING CAMPAIGN

• PLAN AHEAD

Put a date in your diary to stop, and stick to it. Also check out the different stopping strategies in the following chapter. Pick one, none, or a combination of them all. It really doesn't matter. Whatever works for you!

• BIN ALL SMOKING GEAR

Lighters, matches, papers, ashtrays – everything must go.

• DRINK LOADS OF WATER

Helps flush the cigarette toxins from your body.

• STOCK UP ON HEALTHY SNACKS

Cigarettes dull the appetite, but quitting doesn't have to mean you put on weight. You may feel more hungry, but as long as you eat sensibly until the cravings pass your waistline won't suffer.

• EXERCISE, EXERCISE, *EXERCISE!*

Make the most of your new-improved health. Join a gym. Hit the pool. Even little things count, like walking into town instead of slouching on the bus. Anything to fill those lungs and get that heart pumping.

• DON'T BE AFRAID TO GRIEVE

After all, you're giving up something you once enjoyed. If you miss the cigs then admit it. Bottle up your feelings and you'll quickly get bitter about breaking from the pack.

• AVOID SMOKING SITUATIONS

Identify your old lighting up times, and be prepared to see them through without reaching for the ciggies. Also ask your friends to respect your personal air space. At least until you find your feet as a non-smoker.

• ONE DAY AT A TIME

Don't think of going a lifetime without a smoke. Just aim to get through each day. Every second, minute, hour, week and month you go without smoking you're beating the addiction.

• DON'T LOOK FOR EXCUSES

Write down all the reasons why you want to pack in the habit. Then, any time you feel wobbly, whip out your list and remind yourself that there is absolutely no good reason for starting again.

• GET SUPPORT

Asking for help to crack an addiction to nicotine is not an admission of weakness. It's a sign of determination. Turn to family or friends to get you through it, or call Quitline (see p117) and talk things over with a qualified counsellor.

• GIVING IN IS NOT THE END

Should you fall back into bad habits, regard it as a dress rehearsal. Learn from your mistakes, and be better prepared for the next time. The more you try, the better chances you have of succeeding. One day, you will crack it.

• BE POSITIVE

Don't go thinking quitting is just about giving up smoking. Ultimately, it's about regaining all the things you'd lost – from your sense of smell and taste to your sense of self-respect!

STOP CLOCK:

Your body will benefit from the moment you quit smoking. Here's how:

After:

20 minutes:	Blood pressure returns to normal
8 hours:	Oxygen levels in your blood returns to normal
1 day:	Lungs start to clear mucus and smoking debris
2 days:	Your body is officially nicotine-free
3 days:	Easier to breathe and more energy
2-12 weeks:	Circulation improves
3-9 months	Your lungs work better by 10%
5 months	Risk of a heart attack about half that of a smoker
10 years	Risk drops to the same as a lifelong non-smoker

BURNING FACT:

Stub out a 20-a-day habit – save a grand a year.

● QUIZ ●

TIME TO QUIT?

It's easier to get hooked on cigarettes than you think. The habit can creep up on you, even when you reckon you can still take it or leave it. If you've started to enjoy the odd puff, here's how to tell if it's time to reel things in:

1 How important is smoking in your life?

(it isn't) 1 2 3 4 5 6 (it's all that matters)

2 Do you light up a ciggie to change your mood?

(sometimes) 1 2 3 4 5 6 (always)

3 How frequently do you light up?

(every party) 1 2 3 4 5 6 (every hour)

4 How much do you look forward to the next ciggie?

(don't think about it) 1 2 3 4 5 6 (can't think of anything else)

5 Do you ever smoke alone?

(occasionally) 1 2 3 4 5 6 (frequently)

6 How would the prospect of quitting make you feel?

(fine) 1 2 3 4 5 6 (freaked!)

7 A mate confronts you about your smoking habit. How do you react?

(listen and take it on board) 1 2 3 4 5 6 (get defensive)

THE BOTTOM LINE:

If you answered:

0-14 Smoke screen

The odd ciggie may not make you feel like a serious smoker, but the habit can soon catch up with you. Chances are you're only lighting up when other people flash the ash. Heck, you may not even enjoy it!

Advice hit: Act now. Give it up before it becomes a hassle.

15-28 Smoke without fire

At first, you might have sparked up to fit in, but now, you're starting to appreciate the nicotine hit. Perhaps a smoking routine is even starting to take shape. One that could soon rule your life, unless you wake up to what's happening.

Advice hit: You never set out to become a smoker, and it's still not too late to stay true to your word. Look at your reasons for lighting up, and set about getting out of the habit.

29-42 Smoked out

You need regular nicotine to cope with life. Nothing gets in the way of your smoking habit, even though you feel bad about letting things get this far.

Advice hit: Anyone can quit smoking, providing you're clear about your motivation, and you've set yourself a quitting campaign that works for you.

SMOKING STRIFE

Question:

"My dad died last year from cancer. He was a heavy smoker, and his habit almost certainly killed him. It certainly put me off smoking, but I can't seem to get my mates to see sense. Any tips?"

Lawrence, 15

Answer:

When people first start smoking, the long-term health risks often seem too far away to worry about. Having seen what damage cigarettes can cause, you can help by reminding them that no-one is invincible.

Smoking kills, and your experience has obviously been enough to persuade you to steer clear. Share your story with your mates, but don't give up on them just because they carry on.

You can't expect anyone to give up on the spot. All you can do is hope that your tale has sown the seed that will one day persuade them to quit.

Question:

"I smoke roll-ups, but it's turning my fingers yellow. The stain won't scrub off, and it looks really dirty. Any ideas?"

Ali, 15

Answer:

The only effective way to get rid of stains like these is to give up smoking!

The discoloration is caused by the nicotine, tar and other toxins in tobacco smoke. But if you think it looks bad on your fingers, just imagine what it must be doing to your lungs.

What better incentive can you have to quit!

CHAPTER SEVEN

Stopping Strategies

"When I quit, I made my friends promise not to give me any cigarettes, even if I ended up begging them!"

Patty, 15

"The first time I tried to pack in the smokes, I figured I could just stick a nicotine patch on my arm to beat the cravings. How wrong I was! Above all, it takes determination."

Bob, 18

"I didn't think I needed anything to help me give up, until I experienced the reality of going without a smoke! If it wasn't for nicotine chewing gum, I would have been back on the ciggies within days."

Joey, 18

Different people smoke for different reasons. They also give up in different ways. Some feel the need to use an aid to help them quit, while others grit their teeth and go for it. Whatever strategy you choose, only your determination to break free will guarantee success.

Where's your willpower?

If you want to quit, it has to come from the heart. Don't go trying to give up, knowing that you'll probably never make it through the day. Do it when you're determined to go the distance.

Willpower and what else?

Here's the low down on the most popular tried and tested methods to help you give up smoking. Some might appeal more than others, but don't restrict yourself to one method. Tailor your own package, depending on your lifestyle, your habit, and your state of mind. Just be aware that no strategy will work without willpower. It's the magic ingredient. The unshakeable self-belief that you can break free from the habit.

NICOTINE REPLACEMENT THERAPIES (NRT)

While it's the nicotine in cigarettes that makes smoking so addictive, the damage to your health is caused by the tar and poisonous chemicals in the tobacco. Nicotine Replacement Therapy is a process that cuts out the smoking element, but still delivers some of the nicotine hit you crave. The snag is you can't legally buy it until you're 18. Nor will it beat your smoking addiction. Over a period of time, however, it can make withdrawal much easier to handle.

Most forms of NRT are available from chemists, but it's not cheap – costing around £20 a week. For anyone old enough and flush enough to give it a try, be sure to follow the manufacturers instructions and never exceed the recommended use. Otherwise you could end up increasing your nicotine intake, which would make quitting even harder!

Pregnant women, nursing mothers or anyone suffering from high blood pressure or circulation problems should avoid this form of treatment, though health experts agree that it's still better than smoking. Clinically proven to help reducing the number of cigarettes smoked, NRT is available in a number of different forms ...

NAME IT:

Nicotine patches

EXPLAIN IT:

Sticking plasters for smokers. These unlikely-looking aids contain a small amount of nicotine which is absorbed through the skin. Patches come in varying strengths, and can be easily hidden under clothes. Just be aware that the nicotine dose is released steadily and slowly, so it's not going to help you beat a sudden craving.

USE IT:

Instructions vary according to the product. Generally one nicotine patch lasts either 16 or 24 hours, while experts recommend a three month course for maximum effectiveness. As you feel more comfortable without cigarettes, so you should reduce the number of patches. There is a chance that patches can make your skin itchy and red, however, but this can be easily sorted by sticking the patch elsewhere.

SWEAR BY IT:

"After I failed to quit for the third time, my mum suggested I try patches. Seeing that she offered to buy them for me, I figured I should give them a go. At first it felt weird, almost tingly, and I didn't tell anyone what I had stuck on my shoulder. You're not supposed to smoke while using them, and I missed the first few ciggies really badly. Even so, it wasn't such a desperate feeling. I think the patches served to take the edge off things, which was enough to get me through the worst."

Mungo, 18

NAME IT:

Nicotine gum

EXPLAIN IT:

NRT chewy is available in different strengths, and is an effective means of getting you through any sudden need to spark up. When chewed, the nicotine is released into the mouth and swiftly absorbed into the bloodstream. While there's not as much nicotine in a single stick as there is in your average cigarette, it's often enough to get your through those desperate moments.

USE IT:

Experts recommend chewing through no more than 10-15 pieces a day, and then slowly cutting out the habit over a period of three months. Don't overdo it, however, for some chewers report side-effects such as nausea or dizziness.

SWEAR BY IT:

"The first time I tried nicotine gum it left me feeling sick. However, I did chew like a maniac as I was desperate for a fag at the time! Once I'd got used to the bitter taste, and learned to rest the gum in the side of my mouth to let the nicotine absorb more effectively, I found it really useful. In particular it gave my jaw a chance to work off the stress I felt about going without cigarettes."

Nancy, 19

NAME IT:

Nicotine inhalator

EXPLAIN IT:

Recommended for anyone attempting to quit who really misses the habit of sucking on a cigarette. Nicotine inhalators are plastic, and look like cigarette holders. A nicotine capsule can be fitted inside, which delivers the appropriate hit whenever you inhale on the mouthpiece. On average, ten puffs on an inhalator provides the same amount of nicotine as one puff on a cigarette. Ultimately, however, the hit you get is intended as a compliment to the hand-to-mouth action.

USE IT:

Experts recommend using no more than 10-15 cartridges a day, and gradually withdrawing over a three month period. If in doubt, see your GP.

SWEAR BY IT:

"The inhalator saved my life. It helped me give up smoking fairly painlessly, even though my mates laughed whenever I produced it. At first I felt really self-conscious about waving around a flattened tube of white plastic. Some people even thought it was a cigarette holder, but eventually they just left me to get on with it."

Lynsey, 18

NAME IT:

Nicotine Nasal Spray

EXPLAIN IT:

With one squirt into each nostril, a fine spray of nicotine is absorbed into the lining of the nose. It's a very fast and effective way to satisfy a craving, but side effects can include a peppery sensation at the back of the throat, along with some coughing and sneezing.

USE IT:

Unlike other forms of NRT, the nasal spray is only available on prescription. Experts recommend spraying about 10-15 times each day, and then gradually easing off over a three month period. Never sniff or inhale during use.

SWEAR BY IT:

"My eldest brother gave up smoking using the nasal spray, so I hoped it could help me too. The first time I used it left me reeling, however, and I didn't turn to it again for another week. I found the hit to be so strong that it actually left me feeling a little bit sick. Later, when I was going crazy for a ciggie, it was just the turn-off I needed. So I guess it worked for me, but for all the wrong reasons!"

Saul, 18

OTHER METHODS

NAME IT:

Acupuncture

EXPLAIN IT:

A popular alternative therapy, based on ancient Chinese medicine. Treatment involves pricking needles into nerve-sensitive areas of the body to aid healing. While the scientific basis behind acupuncture is still unclear, it is thought to stimulate the brain into releasing a pain-relieving chemical which makes withdrawal from drugs like nicotine much easier to handle.

USE IT:

Acupuncture should only be carried out by a registered practitioner (see p117). Always talk to your doctor first before trying this alternative therapy. Some GP practises now run a free acupuncture service, but you still have to ask for a referral.

SWEAR BY IT:

"My doctor suggested I try acupuncture. I'd had an allergic reaction to nicotine patches, and wanted to try a more natural method of giving up. When she mentioned the needles I was worried it might hurt. No pain, I thought, no gain. Thankfully, I was completely wrong. The hour-long treatment was totally painless, and one of the most relaxing times I'd had in ages. I just sat back and took it easy. Only the tips of the needles get inserted, and I hardly noticed them going in. I can't say it stopped me from wanting to smoke, but it certainly cut back the cravings. I went back for three more sessions, and after that I took up yoga. It's been six months now and I haven't so much as touched a single fag. What's more, the giving-up experience has introduced me to a whole new way of relieving stress!"

Gabrielle, 18

NAME IT:

Hypnosis

EXPLAIN IT:

A treatment that aims to change subconscious beliefs and attitudes which may be stopping a smoker from quitting. Imagine yourself getting counselled while in a dream-like trance, and you get the picture. It's not about mind-control, however, but the power of suggestion. Although the effectiveness of hypnotherapy has yet to be scientifically proven, many ex-smokers have found the treatment useful.

USE IT: *Suite*

Hypnotherapy should only be carried out by a registered practitioner (see p117). Before you try hypnotherapy, consult your GP.

SWEAR BY IT:

"I decided to try hypnosis after I realised that I'd been smoking for most of my teenage years. I chose a group session, and it was comforting to have people around me who were going through the same thing as me. To kick off the therapist took us through some deep breathing and relaxation exercises, so by the time we got to the hypnosis itself we were all deeply chilled. Afterwards, I didn't feel any different, but the way I felt about smoking had changed. I still got cravings, but I felt much more positive about getting through them. I only had two more hypno sessions, and after that I felt strong enough to go it alone."

Roland, 18

NAME IT:

Herbal cigarettes

EXPLAIN IT:

Tobacco-free cigarettes contain a mixture of various herbs such as jasmine, ginseng and clover. It may sound like the ideal solution, but herbal smokes still contain damaging tar and carbon dioxide.

USE IT:

Herbal cigarettes are available from most chemists.

SWEAR BY IT:

"The biggest drawback is the smell. Herbal ciggies are really pungent. They turn heads if you're smoking in public, which can be embarrassing! In some ways it's a good thing, as it meant I thought twice about sparking up. Herbal fags aren't exactly a satisfying smoke, but at least it meant they were easy to quit once I'd got over the nicotine withdrawal from the real thing."

Paul, 16

NAME IT:

Dummy cigarettes

EXPLAIN IT:

Not just nicotine-free, but tar free, carbon-monoxide free too. In fact, there's nothing in a dummy cigarette at all. Purely for those who miss the act of smoking, but not the addiction.

USE IT:

If you can't find a fake fag in the shops then take a biro, remove the guts and you have a dummy cigarette. Just don't try and light it!

SWEAR BY IT:

"I didn't plan to use a dummy cigarette. It was just something a mate gave me as a joke on the first day I quit. In the end, I didn't actually use it much. Most of the time I kept it tucked behind my ear, but it was comforting to know it was there."

Rod, 13

NAME IT:

Covert sensitisation

EXPLAIN IT:

A stopping technique which works by replacing desirable feelings about smoking with negative thoughts. Firstly, imagine you're enjoying a cigarette. Instead of the pleasurable hit you get, however, picture yourself being violently sick. No matter how unpleasant it seems, focus on that nauseous feeling until you actually start feeling ill. Next concentrate on how relieved you feel when you chuck that cigarette away.

USE IT:

Repeat up to 15 times a day, until the very idea of lighting up leaves you feeling queasy.

SWEAR BY IT:

"Covert sensitisation sounds like some flaky hippy method of quitting, but if you're really committed to getting off the smokes it can help. I had to force myself to do the imagination bit every hour of the day for a week. After that I really did feel a bit jippy whenever I thought about cigarettes. I also changed my daily routine to avoid smoking situations, but together it was enough to beat the addiction."

Mercedes, 15

NAME IT:

Rapid smoking (Only use as a last resort!)

EXPLAIN IT:

Smoke until you're sick. How? Take three cigarettes, and get through one after the other. As you work your way through each one, inhale as deeply as you can. At the same time, imagine the damage it's causing inside, and as the carbon monoxide builds up in your circulation think about how good you don't feel. The more pukey you become, the better. After the first three cigarettes, take a five-minute break and repeat. Do this every day for a fortnight, and by the time you're through the very idea of a ciggie will be enough to turn you green.

USE IT:

Rapid smoking can be dangerous. **Always check with your doctor before you try rapid smoking,** just to be sure your body can take the beating.

SWEAR BY IT:

"A friend told me about the rapid smoking technique. The fact that you were encouraged to smoke quickly as a way of giving up really appealed to me, but I wasn't laughing after I tried it. Racing through the first ciggie was a joy, but I didn't feel so good after the second and third. In the break before the next three, I really thought I was going to be throw up. Still, I forced myself to light up the next one, and sure enough it had me praying for mercy over the toilet bowl! It was a disgusting experience, but I made myself repeat the process for another ten days. After that, smoking and me parted company. A pleasant smoke had become torture by tobacco. I wouldn't recommend rapid smoking to everyone, but it worked a treat for me. Nowadays, I can't understand how people smoke without feeling ill."

Rex, 16

THE FUTURE FOR SMOKERS

A drug called Zyban reduces the nicotine craving and makes withdrawal much easier to go through. Previously only available in America, but recently approved in the UK on a prescription-basis from your GP, the drug could be the answer to your nicotine nightmares. The downside? It's only available for smokers aged 18 and over.

10 REASONS TO QUIT:

1. Smoking kills. End of story.

2. Thousands have quit, why can't you?

3. You don't want to be the last person you know to give it up.

4. You're fed up with feeling like a social outcast

5. You don't want to kill anyone through passive smoking.

6. You're sick of smelling like an ashtray

7. You miss having clean white teeth.

8. The extra cash you'd save could come in handy.

9. Cancer? Heart disease? No thanks.

10. When it comes to the deciding factor, wouldn't it be good to say you that you've conquered one of life's most addictive habits?

CHAPTER EIGHT

Staying Smoke Free

"Being a smoker was an experience I never want to repeat."

Seth, 14

"One week after I gave up, I thought I'd never make it. Going without a cigarette was driving me to distraction. I even dreamed about lighting up! It was a tough time, but slowly things got better. Nowadays, I don't even think about smoking. I've got much better things to do with my life!"

Kim, 16

"I'm really proud of myself for giving up smoking. I tried quitting about six times before, and it was only by giving it another go that I finally cracked it."

Nusrat, 15

So you've made the break. Somehow, you found the willpower to want to live your life without tobacco. Right now, you may be feeling thrilled, triumphant and ecstatic. Then again, you could be depressed, irritable and crabbier than a caretaker. Much depends on the stage you've reached in the no-smoking game, just be aware that temptation can rise up at any time. Not least when you think you've cracked it! So whatever you're feeling, stay one step ahead and be prepared to resist it.

KNOW YOUR ENEMY

Nicotine withdrawal hits your mind where it hurts, and your body too. By tinkering with your physical and mental response to a cigarette, the drug fools you into thinking you need to rely on the habit. This means that when you stop sucking nicotine into your system alarm bells start to ring. From the moment you quit smoking, the amount of nicotine in the body drops by half every two hours. This means after 24 hours you are officially nicotine free. In that time, here are some of the physical symptoms that show you're beating the addiction:

- Drop in heart rate and blood pressure
- Difficulty getting to sleep
- Restlessness
- Increased coughing as your lungs start to clear out the rubbish.
- Dry mouth
- Mild sore throat

It takes a little longer to get your head around the idea of not smoking. You're basically giving up a ritual. A regular fix you came to depend upon to feel a certain way. Without it, your mind takes a while to regain the strength to function without fags.

On average it takes about three weeks before the symptoms become easier to manage. In the mean time, here are some of the feelings you could experience:

- Anxiety
- Nervousness
- Tension
- Depression
- Irritability
- Fatigue

BURNING FACT:

On average, the increased appetite associated with quitting cigarettes lasts just under a month. Not long to watch what you eat.

CRUSH THE CRAVING

Giving up cigarettes can be like walking away from a good friend. Without a trusty fag at hand it's easy to get in a spin and think you can't survive without. Just remember that if you invite this so-called-friend back into your life then ultimately it could kill you.

Cravings can be intense, but they also fade fast. If you're able to identify the different situations and feelings before they arise, then you'll be better prepared to stay off the fags. Here's how to get through the worst:

Take Five

No matter how hard
you're hit by a craving,
it will pass quickly. If
you're struck by the urge
to drop everything and search out
a ciggie, why not give yourself five
minutes, and see how you feel then.
In the big scheme of things, five
minutes isn't a long time to wait.
Not when the rest of your life is
at stake.

"The hardest craving to beat is the one that takes
you by surprise. If you're unprepared it's easy to
give in. Whenever I was tempted, I always put off
making the decision for a couple of minutes. It
worked every time. As soon as you step back from
the brink, you find the willpower to push on without
lighting up."

Gina, 16

BURNING FACT:

*If current smoking rates continue, tobacco will kill one
million of today's teenagers in the UK before they
reach middle age.*

Why did I quit?

After packing in the smokes, many people expect to feel a big rush of freedom. Sadly, the reality is often very different. Feelings of depression and doubt can often kick in, especially in the early days as your body grieves its regular nicotine hit. Just don't go thinking that a cigarette will make you feel any better. If anything, lighting up will see your self-respect go up in smoke.

To combat these wobbly moments, it's vital that you remind yourself of all the reasons why you quit. Have them written down somewhere, even on your hand if it helps!

"On the day I quit, my boyfriend sent me a good luck card. I carried it in my bag for weeks. Whenever I got a craving, I only had to read the message inside and I'd feel stronger."

Fiona, 15

BURNING FACT:

71% of teen smokers say they have tried to give up, of which 81% think they will succeed the next time they try.

Relax!

People claim they smoke because it helps beat stress. Not only does this mean you need to find an alternative way to keep cool, you're faced with doing

so while going through the grief of giving up.
Just don't let the tension overtake you.
As soon as you let yourself get wound
up, your old instinct to
reach for the ciggies
returns. Which is only
going to fuel your
tension!

Physical exercise is a good
way to work off stress.
Anything from aerobics to
jogging or a gym session will
sweat out the most extreme nicotine
cravings. Meanwhile, this relaxation
technique will keep you chilled
whenever the call of the ciggies
start winding you up:

- Lie down somewhere
  comfortable and spend
  a minute breathing slowly
  and deeply.
- Next, with your toes pointing downwards, tense
  up the muscles in your feet. Hold for five seconds,
  then relax.
- Now curl your toes upwards and bunch the
  muscles in your ankles. Again, hold for five seconds
  before relaxing.
- Repeat the process on different parts of your body,
  working your way up through your calves, thighs,
  buttocks, stomach, chest, shoulders, neck and even
  the muscles in your face. Finish off by tensing up

your whole body, holding for a final five seconds, and then slowly letting the tension flow out. Feel better? Of course you do!

"It's easy to get tense when you're hungry for a smoke. So many people become uptight in the first few days, and it's often for this reason that they go back to their old ways. After giving in a couple of times, I realised that I had to learn to stay calm if I was ever going to crack it. Swimming really helped me. Not only did it take away the cravings, it gave me time to focus on staying off the cigarettes."

Shaina, 16

BURNING FACT:

57% of young smokers say they plan to give up some time in the future. No time like the present!

Keep busy

Giving up smoking leaves you with time on your hands. Unless you fill it creatively, the cravings will quickly take hold. So be prepared, and always have something up your sleeve to take the place of a ciggie. Whether it's a walk to the newsagent, a phone call to your mate, or a spot of air guitar in your bedroom, make sure you fill that time with something other than a smoke.

"For me, the only way to get over the need for a cigarette was literally by turning my back on the temptation. It meant walking away from my friends whenever they lit up, which was hard but it worked."

Owen, 15

BURNING FACT:

In a recent survey, 91% of smokers aged 15 and under said that mates were their main source of cigarettes. Some friends!

Another step free

Remember, every time you beat a craving you take another step further from the clutches of the addition. Tick it off in your mind, and stay aware that while there may be more obstacles to come they won't be so hard to conquer.

"The first twenty-four hours are the most intense. After that, it's the unexpected craving you have to watch out for. But if you can get through each moment without lighting up, it leaves you with the kind of buzz you could never get from nicotine!"

Phil, 15

BURNING FACT:

17 million cigarettes go up in smoke each week in the UK at the hands of smokers aged 15 and under.

OTHER FLASH POINTS

No matter how well you're prepared, it's impossible to predict the future. Sometimes, smoking scenarios crop up when you least expect them, while events outside your control can seriously test your willpower. Even so, if you really want to quit then nothing life hurls at you will tempt you back to the fags, will it?

Party time!

Even if you plan to keep your social diary empty for the first few weeks of your quitting campaign, the time will come when you'll want to let your hair down.

Staying tobacco-free at a party is tough, especially if in the past you smoked your way from start to finish. If you're determined to stay off the ciggies, however, then get your priorities sorted before you even step out of the house. Promise yourself that you'll take action if the temptation starts to mount. Even if it means going home early, it's got to be worth it in the end. Things won't always be this hard. The more nights out you survive without smoking, the easier it'll become. Besides, at worst, what's one early night in the big scheme of things?

"I gave up smoking six months ago. I'm well over the hard bit, and can go for days without even thinking about cigarettes. Even so, there's still a big temptation to light up at parties. It's the one time when your resolve can fall apart. I gave in once, but I felt so disappointed with myself afterwards that I was never tempted again."

Paul, 15

BURNING FACT:

Smoking may be in decline in rich countries, but in the developing world the number of people who are giving in to the temptation is increasing by 2% each year. In many of these countries, the tobacco manufacturers are not legally obliged to print health warnings on the packets.

Arguments

Everyone gets ratty in the early stages of quitting. It's a natural reaction. All part of the deal while your mind reprograms itself to function without cigarettes. Even if you find yourself surviving on a short fuse, however, don't go taking it out on others. As soon as you start yelling at family and friends, you'll be sparking up to cool off before you know it. If you can avoid the rows, however, you'll also be steering clear of one of the biggest reasons people fall back into the smoking habit:

- Try not to blame your state of mind on the fact that you're quitting. Sure, you're acting a little cranky, but not for much longer.
- Back off from potential flare ups. Don't run away, just give yourself a couple of minutes to calm down, then tackle the issue without shouting.
- If someone has a bone to pick, let them have their say before you respond. Cutting in before they've finished will only raise the temperature between you.
- When things don't go your way, learn to compromise and negotiate an outcome that suits everyone involved.

"My mum said I was a monster for a week after I quit. Luckily she knew the reason why, and gave me the space I needed."

Tuppy, 15

BURNING FACT:

Nicotine has been compared to heroin and cocaine in terms of the drug's addictive potential.

Emotional problems

Relationship difficulties can be hard to handle at the best of times. It's essential that you sort things out by talking the issues through. Don't use tobacco as an emotional crutch. No cigarette ever saved a relationship, or guaranteed happiness at home. Ultimately, smoking is the problem, not the solution.

"I'd given up for a month when I broke up with my boyfriend. In the days that followed I had to fight to stay off the cigarettes. When your emotions take a knock, the temptation to seek reassurance in a smoke is hard to resist. Eventually, things got better when I realised I'd given up two things which were giving me grief!"

Anneka, 16

BURNING FACT:

Research has shown that smokers are about three times as likely to develop eye cataracts than non-smokers.

Over-confidence

At some stage, there'll come a time when you reckon you've cracked the habit. All those cravings will be a thing of the past, and you'll be able to look at a cigarette without coming over all misty-eyed. Just because you've given up, however, don't go thinking you're now immune to the effects of nicotine. Sadly, many ex-smokers feel confident enough to light up again socially, because they mistakenly believe they won't get caught out by the habit.

You may have found the willpower to beat the addiction, but sticking a ciggie in your gob again because you think you're resistant is just asking for trouble. Before you know it, you'll be back to square one. Doh!

> "The feeling is fantastic when you look back and realise you've given up smoking. It's a real rush. Stupidly, I also thought it meant I could handle smoking every now and then without getting addicted. How wrong I was!"
>
> Ellen, 16

BURNING FACT: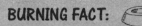

Tobacco advertising in Norway was banned in 1975. Fifteen years later, the number of smokers had dropped by 10%.

A NEW BEGINNING

When does a smoker become an ex-smoker? At what stage can you safely say you've conquered one of the most addictive drugs on the planet? It's a question many people ask themselves, at every stage of the quitting game. Is it one day, a week, a month or a year? How long before you can look people in the eye and say you don't smoke?

The answer? Right from the moment you stub out your last cigarette. Every second you go without lighting up again makes you more of a non-smoker than a smoker. Even if it's hard going to begin with, it'll soon get so much easier. No butts about it!

Summoning up the willpower to quit shows you want to be an individual again. Someone who can go anywhere or do anything without first patting their pockets to check they're alright for ciggies.

So congratulations. If you've got this far then you're no longer a slave to cigarettes. It means no more cash to the tobacco industry, and far less chance of dying early. At last, you can get on with living your life.

You've done it.

You're free.

Useful Contacts

THE INSTITUTE OF CONTEMPORARY MEDICINE
PO Box 194
London SE6 1QZ
Send an sae for further information on acupuncture and hypnotherapy treatment, plus details of registered practitioners local to you.

QUITLINE
0800 00 22 00
Helpline staffed by qualified counsellors. Call as often as you like, for practical help and advice on giving up cigarettes. Lines are open 7 days a week, from 10.00 am to 6.00 pm.

On the web:
ASH
http://www.ash.org.uk
For information on all tobacco issues, including campaigning to reduce addiction, disease and premature death caused by smoking, as well as links to other smoking-related sites.

LIFESAVER
http://www.lifesaver.co.uk
Top site for support, advice and motivation to give up smoking.

MASTER TOBACCO PAGE
http://www.tobacco.org
A good starting point to find info on anything from the history of tobacco to online quitting support groups.

QUESTION IT
http://www.questionit.com
Cutting edge website for any young smoker who doesn't want to be taken for a sucker any longer.

Index

acetone 15
acupuncture 94-95
addiction 9-10, 70
advertising 60-63
alveoli 19
ammonia 28
amputation 22
angina 23
arguments 112
arsenic 28

blood pressure 16, 71, 82, 103
breath 30-31, 72
bronchi 19
bronchioles 19
bronchitis 19-20

cancer 16, 24
carbon monoxide 15, 17-18, 71, 97
chemicals 15-18, 20, 21, 22, 89
contraception 35
covert sensitisation 98
cravings 104-105, 109

dummy cigarettes 97

emphysema 20-21
exercise 80, 107

family 8-9, 41-50, 112-113
fertility 34
formaldehyde 15
friends 7-8, 50-51, 59, 64, 112-113

gum 31

heart 16, 18, 22-23, 35, 44, 82, 103
herbal cigarettes 96-97
hydrogen sulphide 15
hypnosis 95-96

impotence 33

law 36
lead 28
leukaemia 24
lungs 16, 17, 18-21, 82, 103

media 5-6, 60-63
money 37, 67-68, 72
moods 2-4, 9, 113

nicotine gum 91-92
nicotine inhalator 92-93
nicotine nasal spray 93-94
nicotine patches 90-91
NRT (Nicotine Replacement Therapies) 89-94

passive smoking 42-54
phagocytes 20
pregnancy 17, 34-36

quitting 66-67, 69, 70-82,
    88-101

rapid smoking 99-100
reasons 74, 76, 101
relationships 11-13, 52-54, 113

self-esteem 7

senses 73
sex 16, 33-36
skin 28-29, 90
tar 15, 16-17, 89
teeth 32
temptation 57-69, 104-105,
    110-115

weight 4-5, 80
withdrawal 103-104

zyban 100

0208 - 968 78 75 Suad

ORDER FORM
Wise Guides

0 340 71483 2	BULLYING	£3.99
0 340 75297 1	DIVORCE & SEPARATION	£3.99
0 340 69973 6	DRUGS	£3.99
0 340 74411 1	EATING	£3.99
0 340 63604 1	PERIODS	£3.99
0 340 75299 8	SELF-ESTEEM	£3.99
0 340 71042 X	SEX	£3.99
0 340 77842 3	SMOKING	£3.99
0 340 75737 X	SPOTS	£3.99
0 340 74419 7	YOUR RIGHTS	£3.99

All Hodder Children's books are available at your local bookshop or newsagent, or can be ordered direct from the publisher. Just tick the titles you want and fill in the form below. Prices and availability subject to change without notice.

Hodder Children's Books, Cash Sales Department, Bookpoint, 39 Milton Park, Abingdon, Oxon, OX14 4TD, UK. If you have a credit card you may order by telephone - (01235) 400414. Please enclose a cheque or postal order made payable to Bookpoint Ltd to the value of the cover and allow the following for postage and packing:

UK & BFPO – £1.00 for the first book, 50p for the second book, and 30p for each additional book ordered, up to a maximum charge of £3.00.
OVERSEAS & EIRE – £2.00 for the first book, £1.00 for the second book, and 50p for each additional book.

Name ....

Address ....

....

....

If you would prefer to pay by credit card, please complete the following:
Please debit my Visa/Access/Diner's Card/American Express (delete as applicable) card no:

----- ----- ----- ----- ----- ----- ----- ----- ----- ----- ----- ----- ----- ----- ----- -----

Signature ....

Expiry Date ....